The bell rang from the Chapel while we walked.
Oh, where are autumn days and nights like these!
I showed my friend the tower above the Hill,
And Capen Path, Ballou between the trees.
A gate in the Fence showed faintly in the dusk.
In East and West the lights began to shine.
A group of men passed by and called, "Hullo —"
My heart sang, and I thought, "My college —
mine!"
The Row in autumn twilight! Tall dark trees
Leaned kindly over us. We talked of games,
But I remembered old familiar friends,
And I was silent, thinking of old names.
The men who walked the Row before my time
Were by my side, good ghosts my thought
awoke —
While I must show my friend the tennis court,
The newest hall for men, the gym. He spoke:
"How you must love this place!" My heart stood still
And ached to think how much I love this Hill.

Professor John Holmes A29, H62, from "Along the Row"

Overleaf: Carmichael Hall

Portico, Ballou Hall

TUFTS
UNIVERSITY

PHOTOGRAPHED BY ROBERT AZZI

HARMONY HOUSE
PUBLISHERS LOUISVILLE

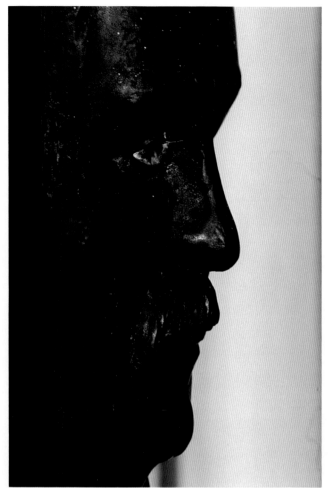

Bas relief, Austin B. Fletcher, LL.D., Ballou Hall

Executive Editors: William Butler and William Strode
Library of Congress Catalog Number: 87-083181
Hardcover International Standard Book Number 0-916509-47-8
Printed in USA by Gateway Press, Louisville, Kentucky
First Edition printed Fall, 1988 by Harmony House Publishers,
P.O. Box 90, Prospect, Kentucky 40059 (502)228-2010 / 228-4446
Copyright © 1988 by Harmony House Publishers
Photographs Copyright © 1988 by Robert Azzi

The publishers wish to thank Tufts University Alumni Relations Director Ron Brinn, A58,
and Associate Director Sandra Ciolfi, J60, and Tufts University Alumni Association
President, Robert A. Sears, A50, M54, and immediate past President Sheila
McDermott, J57, for their assistance and guidance in the production of the book.
We also want to thank Professor Emeritus Russell E. Miller, H83, University
Archivist, and Robert Johnson-Lally, Associate Archivist, for their help in
the research of the historical photographs in this book.

Cabot Intercultural Center, The Fletcher School of Law and Diplomacy

The Memorial Steps

PREFACE

This book makes vivid what Tufts' alumni already know: We have become a regional, national and international university. Our students and faculty learn, teach, and work in many lands besides the United States. Our graduates live all over the world. One of our four campuses is in the French Alps, at Talloires on beautiful Lake Annecy. Our Health Sciences campus occupies twelve acres in busy downtown Boston; the Veterinary School's 600-acre campus lies in the green hills of central Massachusetts.

Tufts University has achieved what our first president, Hosea Ballou, prophesied for his college: "a source of illumination, as a beacon standing on a hill, where its light cannot be hidden, its influence will naturally work like all light; it will be diffusive." But for the great majority of the Tufts community, the campus where Charles Tufts set his light in 1852 is still the heart of the University. The trees, given in our early years by generous citizens of Medford and Somerville and Universalists from around the state, tower where sheep once cropped the grass. Tufts' buildings — some beautiful, all cherished by the Tufts community — share the Hill with its trees. Both symbolize the "greening" of the University with the intellectual life of generations of faculty and students. And each year members of the Tufts family come home to the campus where Ballou Hall was once classroom, dormitory, and administrative office for four professors, seven students, and one president.

Jean Mayer

INTRODUCTION

In the mid-19th century, the friends of Charles Tufts, founding benefactor of Tufts College, called the place that we celebrate in these pages "that bleak hill over in Medford," thereby eliciting from him his famous promise to "put a light on it."

In the mid-1980s, the publishers of *Barron's Profiles of American Colleges* described the same spot as the site of one of thirty-six of the most competitive insitutions of higher learning in the country.

In between, Tufts poet John Holmes called it "the kingdom I was looking for," President Jean Mayer repeatedly called it "either the smallest complex university in the country or the most complex small university in the country," and early trustee P.T. Barnum, if he had been asked to call it anything at all, might have called it The Greatest Show on Earth.

And, for part of their lives, more than 60,000 alumni called it home.

The reality of Tufts is as diverse as their experiences of it, and to define its essence adequately would require reliving 60,000 separate Tufts experiences.

Instead, photographer Robert Azzi spent several months making periodic visits to today's Tufts, compiling a melange of images that at best can suggest the spirit of the institution. As you meander through these pages, you may experience a moment of recognition, shed a tear at a poignant memory, smile at the scene of a past frivolity, or feel yourself quicken with curiosity about a part of Tufts you have never seen.

The Hill

The spirit of Jumbo haunts the Hill campus. Tufts' ponderous mascot was originally personified in the actual stuffed hide of the largest African elephant ever captured. The famed pachyderm was killed in a train crash in Ontario in 1885. The skin of the 12-foot-high circus star was presented to Tufts as the centerpiece for the Barnum Museum of Natural History in Barnum Hall. Jumbo, alas, was destroyed in a 1975 fire, making it impossible for future generations of Tufts students to gain luck in exams by placing pennies in his trunk or pose for pictures in his shadow. But Jumbo's enduring influence is evident in a glance around campus, where his likeness is seen on sweatshirts and stuffed toys, pennants and paperweights, and where Homecoming is highlighted by a procession of papier mache pachyderms. A contemporary elephant statue even squirts water into a fountain nestled within the courtyard of Wessell Library.

Beyond the elephant footprints, though, the Hill campus is marked by figurative footprints of generations of Tufts students and professors who have given the institution its character.

Those who traverse the western end of the Carmichael quad today, smelling the pungent odor of freshly fertilized lawn in spring, seldom remember that they are walking on the former site of a three-million gallon reservoir on whose banks students past courted and cavorted.

Those who cut downhill on the footpath that leads from the side of Richardson House on Professors Row to Cohen Auditorium, (now part of Henry J. Leir Hall) on Talbot Avenue in summer little realize that they tread in the footsteps of Navy V-12 cadets of the 1940s, Tufts Mayoral Campaign candidates of the '50s, and anti-Vietnam protesters of the late '60s and early '70s.

Those who assemble for freshman matriculation near Ballou Hall and the President's House in the Fall may not be aware that Tufts' first freshman class, seven members strong, matriculated inside Ballou Hall — where they also attended classes, slept, ate, used library facilities and worshipped at chapel; for in 1854 it was the sole campus building.

Those who taste the Tufts international flavor as they pass through the Cabot Intercultural Center's hall of flags do not often hear the echo of Professor Leo Gross's voice teaching the tenets of international law to generations of U.S. and foreign diplomats at the Fletcher School.

Those who shudder with a piercing wind that cuts across the top of the Hill in winter may not remember alumnus poet John Ciardi's chilling observation that "Tufts rises high on a drumlin, a pocket of till fallen from a frayed glacier. Had the ice sprawled a few miles southeast for the letting go, the Hill might have been an island in Boston Harbor."

The campus, which might for that trick of prehistoric fate have been a topological island, instead became an intellectual one — a 153-acre area that is part of the Medford and Somerville communities, and yet separates itself from them by virtue of having its own traditions, its own culture, its own governance. Through such programs as the Eliot-Pearson Children's School, the Tufts Day Care Center, community nights at the Tufts Arena Theater in summer, and the Leonard Carmichael Society's annual Kids' Day carnival, it enriches its larger environs.

But only those who actually have spent their days, weeks, and years on the Hill really know the feeling of sitting on the library roof watching the lights of Boston twinkle on, having a class move impulsively out of a century-old, ivy-covered building and onto the lawn to soak up the Hilltop sun, or hearing the bells in the Goddard Chapel tower toll at midnight on Commencement eve to welcome each year's new graduates into the alumni body.

On the Green

Goddard Chapel

Only those who have thrilled to the feeling of rowing a Tufts shell along the Charles River, burned the midnight oil pasting up copy for the *Tufts Weekly*, the *Tufts Observer* or the *Tufts Daily*, or heard tales of Tufts' past told by Professors Russell Miller and Russell Carpenter or cheered the Jumbos football team to an autumn victory against Williams or Amherst can feel appropriately stirred by the sounds of the Beelzebubs singing "Tuftonia's Day" a cappella.

Only those who have thrown eggs out of a classroom window as part of an engineering design experiment, who have stayed up all night checking light cues or striking a set for a Pen, Paint and Pretzels production, who have probed the serious problem of world hunger at the School of Nutrition, or helped a handicapped person gain skills for everyday living through knowledge acquired at the Boston School of Occupational Therapy, can appreciate the diversity of the Tufts experience.

Only those whose memories include things like the disarray on the Hill the morning after the 1938 hurricane, Robert Frost reading his own poetry in Goddard Chapel on a snowy evening, field trips with geology professors Bob Nichols or Charlie Stearns or archaeological digs in Sardinia with Miriam Balmuth, lunch or bridge and coffee at the Kursaal, athletic events where Medford mailman Bob Winn infused the crowds with Jumbo spirit, Spring Sings in Cousens Gym, or the contagious enthusiasm of Tufts professors can truly be said to have seen that light on the Hill.

Beyond the Drumlin

Of course, Tufts is more than the Hill campus. Joint degree programs find undergraduates enrolled in courses at Boston's New England Conservatory of Music, and both undergrads and graduate alumni recollect studio courses at the world-acclaimed School of the Museum of Fine Arts as a highlight of their Tufts experience. In recent years, hundreds of undergraduates have also chosen to enroll in Tufts programs abroad — many of them at the university's own European campus in the medieval village of Talloires, France, on the banks of beautiful Lake Annecy, just outside Geneva. Those who have walked the paths of Talloires, sat in classes in the ancient Benedictine priory that is the Tufts European Center, and explored the surrounding Haute Savoie countryside, with its beauty and its sense of history, will never be able to remember Tufts without that French accent.

To many alumni, the experience of Tufts centered on the health sciences campuses. The images that the name of alma mater evokes for them include the exhilaration of learning from many of the medical profession's foremost practitioners, the thrill and terror of the first surgical experience, the hours spent in laboratories or in clinics. For medical and dental graduates, the memories include passing among the tall buildings near the edge of Boston's Chinatown among other men and women with white jackets, learning how to communicate with patients, filling a first tooth, taking a dental impression, working long nights in hospital rotations, and eagerly awaiting word of where residencies will be performed. Other health professionals will remember working on advanced research projects at Tufts' Sackler School of Graduate Biomedical Sciences, or on pioneering studies at the U.S. Department of Agriculture Human Nutrition Research Center on Aging at Tufts. For those who have attended Tufts' veterinary school, recollections include scenes of pastoral beauty in rural Grafton — pasture land and barns and a hospital where patients can include not only cats and dogs, but farm animals, race horses, red-tailed hawks, polar bears, llama and wounded osprey, and where the dividing line between human and animal health concerns is blurred.

There are many, many causes for celebration of the worldwide holiday, Tuftonia's Day. Drift through the pages of this book and recall some.

THERESA PEASE
Tufts University Alumni Association
Service Citation Recipient, 1987

A TUFTS CHRONOLOGY

1852 Charter issued to Trustees of Tufts College, representing the first venture into higher education of the Universalist Church. Tufts was 163rd institution of higher education chartered in the United States. Charter prohibits a religious test for either faculty or students.

1853 Rev. Hosea Ballou 2nd agrees to serve as the first President; Cornerstone laid for the college building (later Ballou Hall), on 20 acres of land donated by Charles Tufts.

1854 Tufts College opens with seven students and four professors.

1855 A second building constructed to serve as a dormitory. Initially known as West Hall, it was renamed Middle Hall in 1886 and served as the college library. Finally, in 1910, it was renamed Packard Hall in honor of Silvanus Packard, an early and important benefactor of the college.

1857 First Commencement, with three students graduating.

1860 East Hall dormitory constructed; Tufts Alumni Association formed.

1862-1864 Alonzo Ames Miner elected President; Reservoir for Charlestown constructed on hilltop.

1865-1866 Baseball opens intercollegiate sports with loss to Brown; (Football introduced in 1874/75); Three-year program in Civil Engineering introduced.

1869 A Divinity School is started (later to be named Crane Theological School).

1872 West Hall constructed.

1875 Elmer Hewitt Capen elected President. Enrollment totals 56, exclusive of the Divinity School.

1878 Charter amendment raises number of Trustees from 23 to 30.

1879 Total enrollment, 102.

1881-1882 Goddard Chapel completed.

1884 Barnum Museum of Natural History constructed.

1887 Dean Hall dormitory constructed. (Razed in 1963 for Fletcher expansion.)

1891-1892 Trustees vote to admit women to undergraduate programs; first female graduate receives degree on 1893; Paige and Miner halls constructed to serve as headquarters and dormitory for the Divinity School.

1893 Medical School opened with 80 students enrolled; Metcalf Hall built as dormitory for women.

1894 "Permanent appointments" to faculty recognized by President Capen; Commons building constructed, later renamed Curtis Hall.

1894-1895 Mechanical Engineering Department founded.

1899 Tufts Dental School founded; Robinson Hall constructed; Howe Laboratory (foundry and heating plant) constructed (razed in 1960 for Anderson Hall).

1900 A new building was constructed on Huntington Avenue in Boston to house the Medical and Dental Schools, at a cost of $167,000.

1901 First Tufts Night at Pops.

1905 President Capen dies; Frederick William Hamilton elected and takes office in 1906 after serving as Acting President in 1905.

1908 New library, gift of Andrew Carnegie, ready but unopened for two years for lack of operating funds; named for Reverend Charles Eaton at request of Mrs. Carnegie.

1910 Charter change creates separate Jackson College for Women, opened with 54 students from the College of Letters, 6 transfers, 2 special students, and 23 new students.

1912 President Hamilton resigns; Professor William L. Hooper (Engineering) named Acting President.

1914 Hermon Carey Bumpus elected President.

1915 American Radio and Research (AMRAD) was incorporated, and constructed a wireless station with elevated antenna in building later to be named North Hall.

1916 Anatomy building constructed adjacent to Huntington Avenue property; enlarged in 1917 and again in 1920.

1917-1918 College shifts to war footing; President Bumpus working in Washington; war emergency courses for civilians; establishment of the Student Army Training Corps units.

1918 President Bumpus resigns; John Albert Cousens named Acting President, and as President in 1920.

1923 Pearson Chemistry building constructed; major bequest from Board Chairman Austin B. Fletcher, Class of 1876, intended to found School of Law and Diplomacy.

1926 Fletcher Hall constructed.

1927 Stratton Hall, a Dormitory for Women, opened.

1931-1932 Gymnasium built, later to be named for President Cousens.

1933 The Fletcher School of Law and Diplomacy opens in remodeled Goddard Gym, with 21 students and an enrollment limit of 50.

1937 President Cousens dies; Dean George S. Miller named Acting President.

1938 Leonard Carmichael elected President. President's House built. Joseph H. Pratt Diagnostic Clinic and Hospital founded as a part of the New England Medical Center.

1941 Navy R.O.T.C. unit established at Tufts.

1943 Navy V-12 program initiated, with 1,000 trainees on campus.

1944 Reservoir on Hill turned over to college by Metropolitan District Commission, dismantled and filled in.

1945 With veterans 80% of undergraduate colleges, Stearns Village constructed to house married students; affiliation established with School of the Museum of Fine Arts and the Boston School of Occupational Therapy.

1947 Ph.D. programs reauthorized in Arts and Sciences.

1948 Bookstore (Taberna) and Jackson Gym for Women constructed in Medford. Overcrowding in Eaton Library, as collection grows past 150,000 volumes. War Memorial Wing added in 1950.

1949 Forming of Air Force ROTC

1949-1950 Medical and Dental Schools move to Harrison Avenue.

1951 Construction started on Posner Hall dormitory for Boston students; affiliation with Nursery Training School (later named Eliot-Pearson).

1952 Construction of major dorm in Medford, later named for President Carmichael. Construction of Cohen Auditorium and Alumnae Hall in 1954, linking Jackson Gym and Cohen.

1953 President Carmichael resigns. Professor Nils Yngve Wessell named Acting President. President in 1953-54.

1954 Construction of Hodgdon Hall; establishment of Lincoln Filene Center for Citizenship and Public Affairs.

1955 Change of name from Tufts College to Tufts University, retaining corporate identity of Trustees of Tufts College.

1959-1962 Construction of Dewick Hall, 1959; Bush Hall, 1959; Tilton Hall, 1961-62.

1960 Formal adoption of brown and blue colors used informally but without definition of shade since 1878.

1961 Major revision of the undergraduate curriculum.

1963-1965 Construction of Mugar Hall and renovation of Goddard Hall for the Fletcher School.

1964 Tufts takes over Bouve buildings as Hill Hall and Lane Hall; creation of the Experimental College.

1965 Construction of Wessell Library.

1966 President Wessell resigns; Professor Leonard C. Mead named Acting President.

1967 Burton Crosby Hallowell elected President.

1969 Construction of Lewis Hall dormitory.

1971 North Hall gutted by fire.

1973 Construction of Dental Health Sciences Tower and of Proger Building for the New England Medical Center Hospital.

1975 Barnum fire: loss in fire of elephant Jumbo, Tufts mascot, donated by P.T. Barnum, an original Trustee, in 1880s; Construction of Eliot-Pearson Curriculum Research Laboratory.

1976 President Hallowell resigns; Jean Mayer elected President.

1978-1979 Completion of Barnum Hall reconstruction and expansion. Gift of Priory at Talloires, France, and inception of special programs there.

1979 Inception of 140,000,000 Campaign for Tufts; School of Veterinary Medicine opens with an enrollment of 41 students.

1980-1981 Creation of Sackler School of Graduate Biomedical Sciences and the School of Nutrition; opening of Latin Way dormitory.

1981-1982 Opening of the Cabot Intercultural Center at the Medford campus and the Large Animal Hospital at the Grafton campus; opening of Hillside dormitory.

1982-1983 Opening of the Human Nutrition Research Center on Aging.

1985 Opening of the Elizabeth Van Huysen Mayer Campus Center; successful completion of five-year $145,000,000 Capital Campaign; creation of the Center for Environmental Management; the Henry and Lois Foster Small Animal Hospital opened on Grafton campus; Tuftonia's Day established as annual holiday.

1986 Dedication of the Arthur M. Sackler Center for Health Communications in Boston.

1987 Inauguration of $250,000,000 capital campaign.

Near Boston town,
there's a good old hill
Where they turn out stock
from a knowledge mill
Here's to good old Tufts,
the Brown and Blue.

E. W. Newton, '90, in
"Aren't You Glad"

19

Here generations of Tufts men have lived their brief
four years, perhaps in the very rooms their fathers
occupied before them. Here still linger the traditions of
historic "rough houses" and "hoodangs" of by-gone
days. Today the life in the old dormitory is much the
same, and the pleasantest memories of many a young
man are linked with high ungainly rooms and the bleak,
wind-swept hallways of West.

Here and There at Tufts, 1909

Nils Y. Wessell Library

The Library, circa 1910

Yes, I am proud to be President of Tufts. I can say to you what John Albert Cousens, our sixth President, said to Harold Sweet, President of his Board of Trustees, "Our view must reach far into the future; within the field of our endeavor there must be no limit to our ambition....we are rich with the riches most to be prized; rich in men and women, you will find them everywhere among the students, among the alumni, on the staff, in the Board of Trustees; men and women ready to grapple with each problem as it comes, and to solve it finally." Day by day, my faith in our University strengthens.
Jean Mayer, Inaugural Address, September 18, 1976

The freshman cap, circa 1930s

*There was an ambiance about the Tufts I remember
which, if romanticized, is not unlike that of Camelot.
Permeating the campus was an atmosphere of civility
and friendship.*

Allan D. Callow, M.D., A38, G48, G52, H87, in
High on the Hill

Overleaf: The Memorial Steps

Tufts rises on a drumlin, a pocket of till
fallen from a frayed glacier. Had the ice
sprawled a few miles southeast for the letting-go
the Hill might have been an island in Boston Harbor,
had rip tides let it be till piles could shore it
firm to the map.

John Ciardi, A38, H60, from *The Highest Place in Town*

Nobel Laureate Physicist Allan M. Cormack

Testing in the new Navy R.O.T.C. program, 1941

"Young man...buildings do not make a college."
That truth has been stamped ineffaceably upon my
mind with the lapse of years. Indeed, I may go
further, and declare that the Alma Mater of your
love does not consist in its buildings, its labora-
tories, its facilities of whatever sort, nor even in its
living body of wise and learned teachers, but in the
great company of the children whom it has trained.

President Elmer Hewitt Capen, baccalaureate
sermon, June, 1895

Outside Anderson Hall

Philosopher of Mind, Dr. Daniel C. Dennett

Tufts unique role is and will be that of a small university of high quality. As a university it assembles a faculty and a student body representative of a rich and broad range of man's intellectual interests and accomplishments...The number of small universities of high quality is few — number them if you can. Our most important trust is to guard and retain that role, to resist the easy temptation of bigness, and to strengthen instead the richness and the personal nature of our students' intellectual experiences.

President Nils Y. Wessell, installation address, December 9, 1953

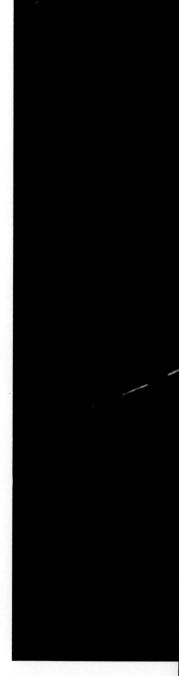

One youth comes up and asks the college to give him wealth, another to give him position, another to give him power, another to give him knowledge.. And the college, wise with the lives of her children, looks deep into their eyes and says, "You know not what you ask." Her highest ideal for you is in an educated man, by which I mean a man in whose training there have been no oversights, who is cultivated as well as learned, who has pure manners as well as fine skill, who has high moral character as well as great powers.

Professor Thomas Whittemore, '94, address to undergrads, 1902

Goddard Chapel

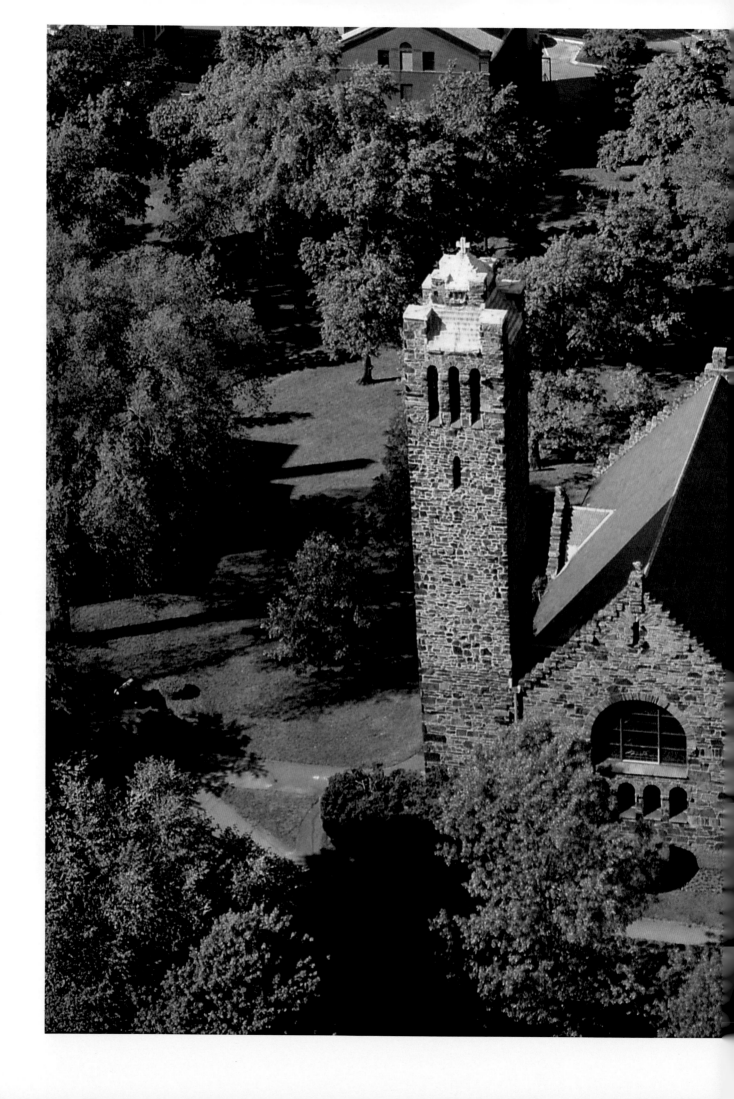

Stately Manor, President's House

Students pose on the lawn of East Hall, circa 1871

Spring on the Hill is sweeter far
Than springs before or after are.
The time will come, for time's old reason,
When spring will be — another season.
Remember then, remember well,
The curving paths, the chapel bell,
And think of mornings when the sun
Lighted your windows one by one;
Of how the trees arched overhead
To shade the Row; how shadows spread
A dappled pattern on the grass
Where you went by with books for class.
Call back the memories you made
Of where you lived and loved and played
Four mays, four Aprils, and four Junes,
And countless drowsy afternoons.
Remember most of all the trees,
And then their murmuring in the breeze;
The ivy by the window stirring;
The hard impatient whirring;
The green sweet smell of grass and sun;
The roads that like a ribbon run...
Remember any April day,
And many a moonlit night, and say,
"Spring on the Hill is sweeter far
Than springs before or after are."

Professor John Holmes, A29, H62

The "Rez," circa 1874

Elizabeth van Huysen Mayer Campus Center

45

Women's track

Center Stage, Cohen Auditorium, Leir Hall

Allan D. Callow Rare Book Room, School of Medicine

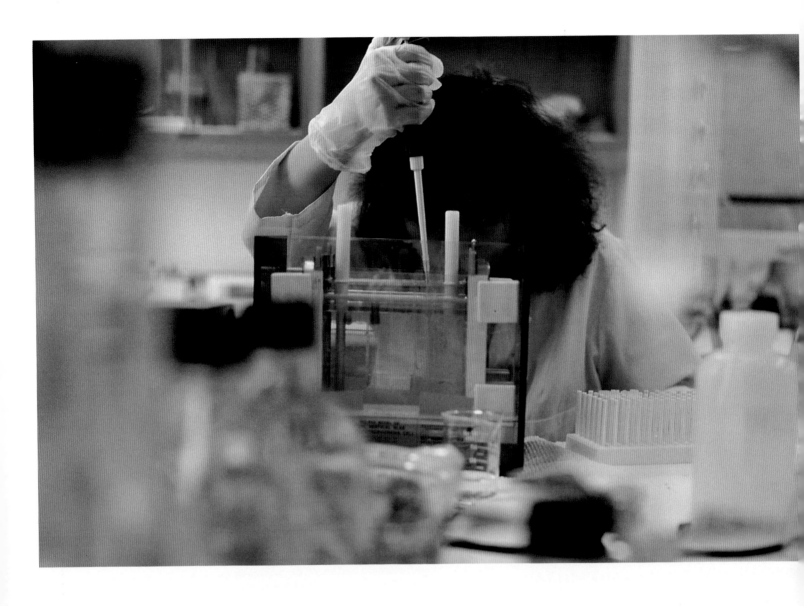

There has been a growing realization within the university that Tufts is doing different things, that w[e] are doing them very well, that several of our school[s] are the best in the country, and that we have certai[n] dimensions that are uncommon if not unique among American universities. We are more and more recognized by the best of the world as a national institution.

President Jean Mayer, in Tufts *Criterion*, Winter 1983

The Medical - Dental Building, circa 1900

Arthur M. Sackler Center for Health Communications

School of Dental Medicine

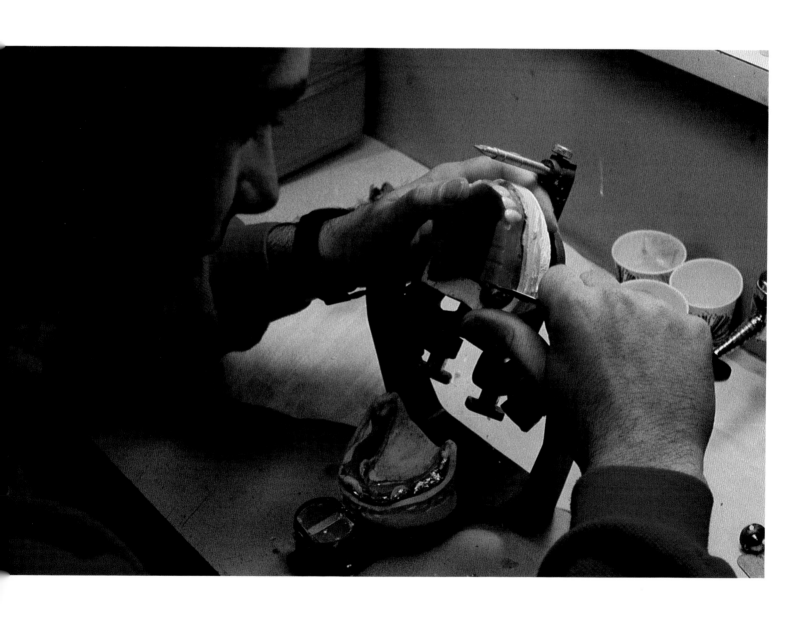

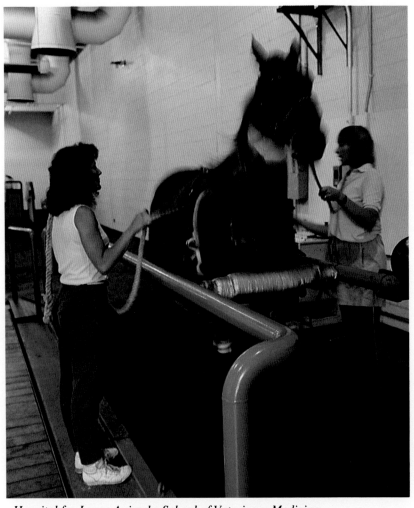

Hospital for Large Animals, School of Veterinary Medicine

Henry and Lois Foster Hospital for Small Animals, School of Veterinary Medicine

Dr. Johanna Dwyer, School of Nutrition

Panorama from Cabot Intercultural Center

Navy V-12 program initiated, with 1000 trainees on campus

Annual Pass In Review, NROTC Midshipmen

Cousens Gymnasium

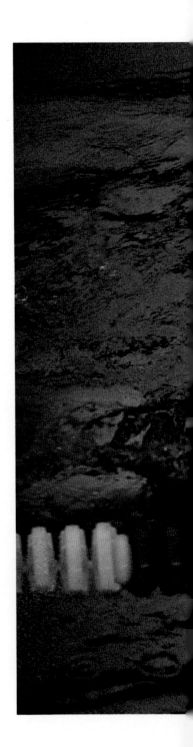

Tufts football team, 1893

Hamilton Pool

Ellis Oval Complex

Tufts basketball team, circa 1925

Jumbo Stampede, The Homecoming Games

Women's Field Hockey, 1924

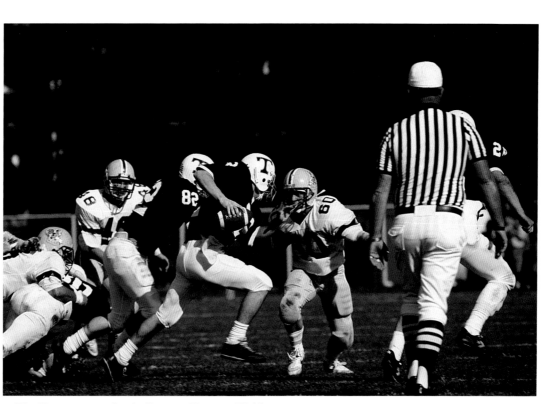

The Homecoming football game, Zimman Field

Jackson Jills

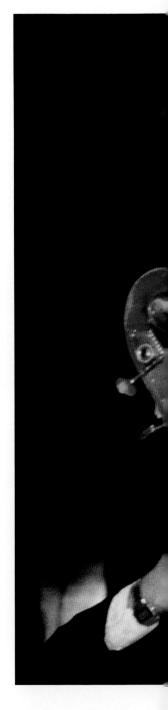

The start of school in 1940

Hail and Farewell Party, Alumni Weekend

Men's chorale, 1920s

Alumni Weekend

Jumbo the elephant placed in Barnum Hall, 1889

Bendetson Hall (formerly University Store)

Paige/Miner Arcade

Miner Hall

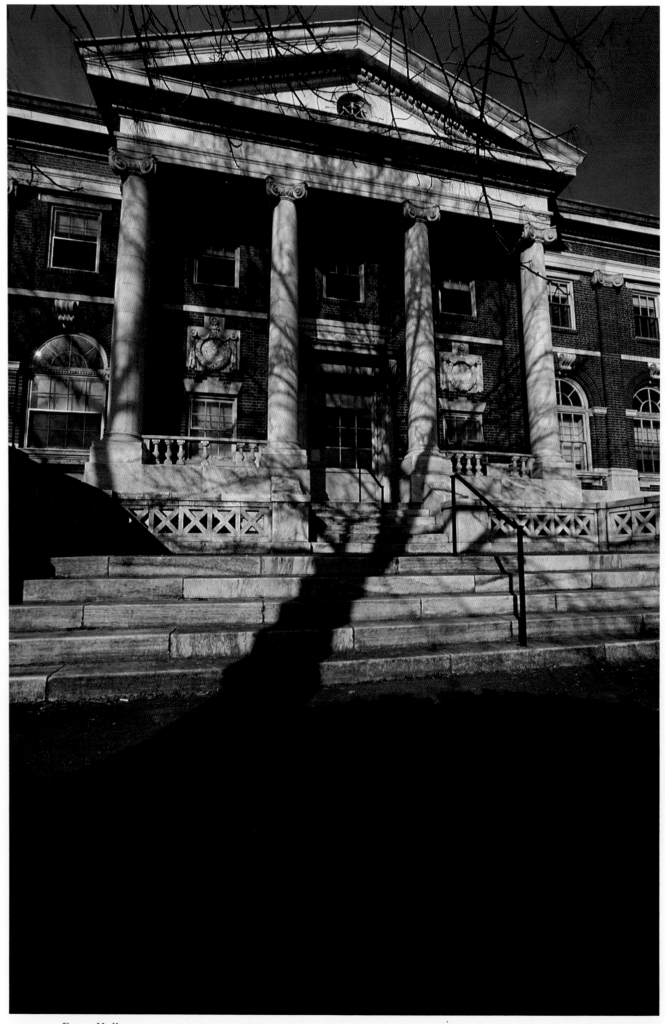

Eaton Hall

For if Tufts College is to be a source of illumination, as a beacon standing on a hill where its light cannot be hidden, its influences will naturally work like all light; it will be diffusive.

President Hosea Ballou 2nd, 1855

Ballou Hall

Barnum Hall fire, 1975

Our sons shall go down Professor's Row,
And stroll on the campus green.
With song and jest they'll find the best
Of the life we once have seen.
Only the names of their friends will be changed
From names we knew on the hill...

Eugene Eaton Smith, A26

THIS IS THIS WORLD, THE KINGDOM I WAS LOOKING FOR
John Holmes

John Holmes A29, H62 Memorial

91

Delt doorway, Fraternity Row

*Previous page: Top O' The
Hill Tribute, Alumni Weekend*

Dr. Jean Mayer, Commencement

Opening Convocation, circa 1920s

This university holds a special place in the history of education in this country. Its "light on the hill for all to see" has illumined the advance of science and the arts for more than a century, and you who are graduated from it today join a procession of contributors, a parade of great meaning, to the advancement of our fellow man that extends far beyond today's line, back through the whole train of our country's history.

Howard W. Johnson, President M.I.T., commencement address, June, 1967

Your Alma Mater brings you good cheer. She bids you place before you the very highest attainment, and work towards it with unflagging purpose. She gives the stamp of her approval to what you have already done. She promises to follow you with friendly interest to the end of your several careers. She will be with you, by her all-powerful instruction, in every step of your mysterious journey.

President Elmer Hewitt Capen, commencement address, June 18, 1893

Carmichael Cupola

*We left on the 1:30 train, and I bid a farewell to College Hill
with all its pleasant scenes and memories. I was sorry to
leave. It was all very fine indeed.*

Elmer Danforth Colcord, A17, C19, in *Very Fine Indeed!*